Would You You Rather?

Dirty Edition

WOULD YOU RATHER?

Go toe to nose

OR

toe to toe with your partner?

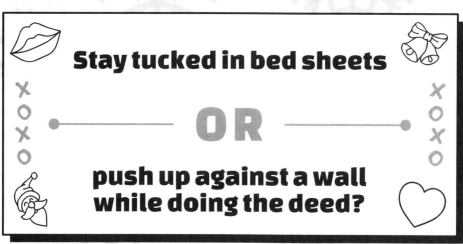

Stay tucked in bed sheets

OR

push up against a wall while doing the deed?

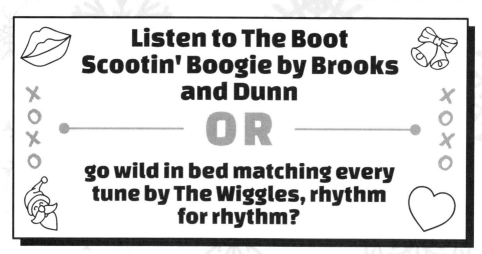

Listen to The Boot Scootin' Boogie by Brooks and Dunn

OR

go wild in bed matching every tune by The Wiggles, rhythm for rhythm?

WOULD YOU RATHER?

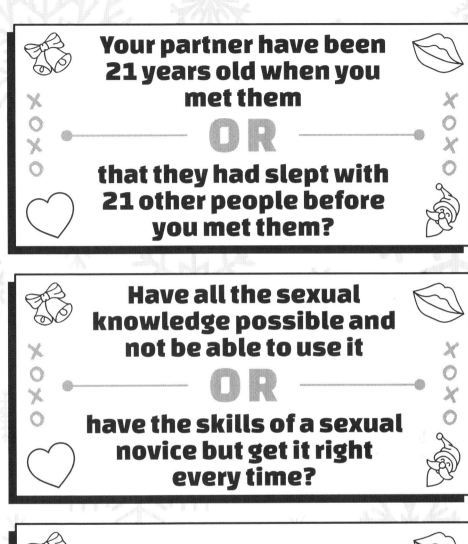

Your partner have been 21 years old when you met them

OR

that they had slept with 21 other people before you met them?

Have all the sexual knowledge possible and not be able to use it

OR

have the skills of a sexual novice but get it right every time?

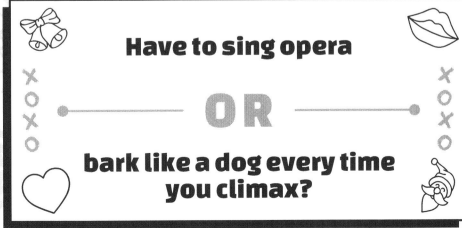

Have to sing opera

OR

bark like a dog every time you climax?

WOULD YOU RATHER?

Spend a sweaty, messy sex-capade outdoors on the hottest day of summer

OR

"Netflix and chill" but feel intensely cold as you get down and dirty?

Stub your toe and orgasm after the initial pain

OR

orgasm every time you accidentally trip?

Skinny dip in a public pool along with a bunch of people you know

OR

at a nude beach with strangers you'll never meet again?

WOULD YOU RATHER?

Drink 20 shots of tequila in one go

OR

kiss an ex?

Lick your partner's cheek

OR

kiss their feet?

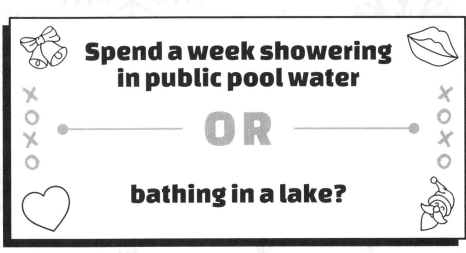

Spend a week showering in public pool water

OR

bathing in a lake?

WOULD YOU RATHER?

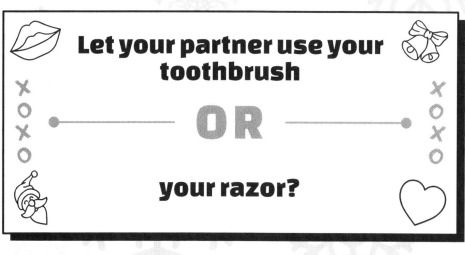

Let your partner use your toothbrush

OR

your razor?

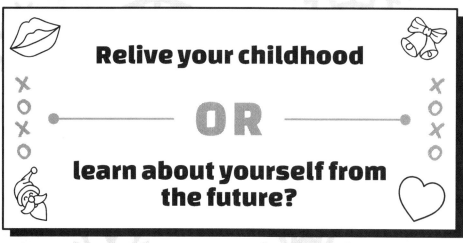

Relive your childhood

OR

learn about yourself from the future?

Have children who are just like your parents

OR

just like your partner's parents?

WOULD YOU RATHER?

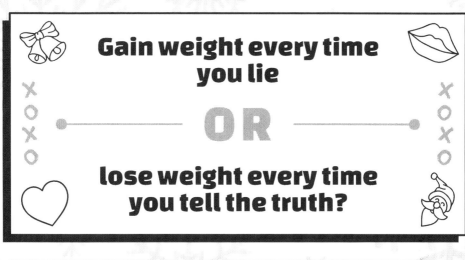

Gain weight every time you lie

OR

lose weight every time you tell the truth?

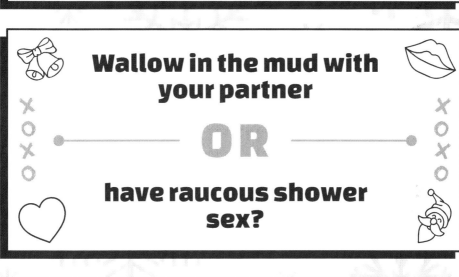

Wallow in the mud with your partner

OR

have raucous shower sex?

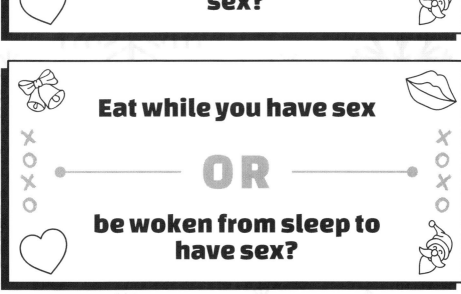

Eat while you have sex

OR

be woken from sleep to have sex?

WOULD YOU RATHER?

Have the perfect body, but everyone knows what you look like naked

OR

have an average body and keep your anonymity?

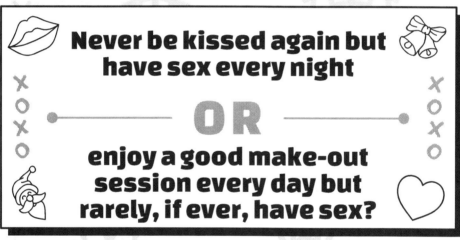

Never be kissed again but have sex every night

OR

enjoy a good make-out session every day but rarely, if ever, have sex?

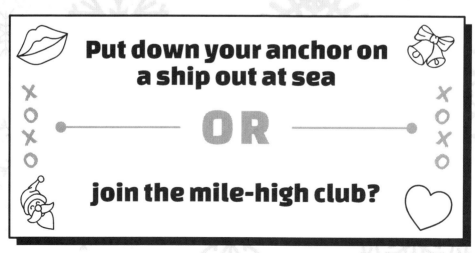

Put down your anchor on a ship out at sea

OR

join the mile-high club?

WOULD YOU RATHER?

Have everyone hear what's going on behind closed doors

OR

get caught having sex in public?

Have sex in an isolated but small car

OR

inside a large dressing room in a crowded mall?

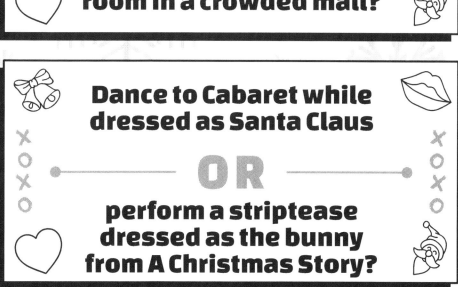

Dance to Cabaret while dressed as Santa Claus

OR

perform a striptease dressed as the bunny from A Christmas Story?

WOULD YOU RATHER?

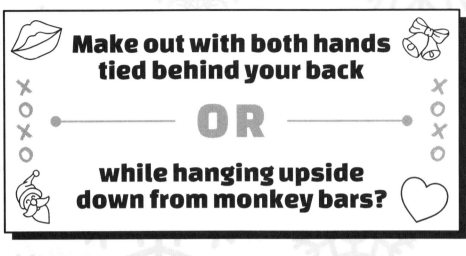

Make out with both hands tied behind your back

OR

while hanging upside down from monkey bars?

Prank call your ex

OR

hold a spicy chili under your tongue for an entire minute?

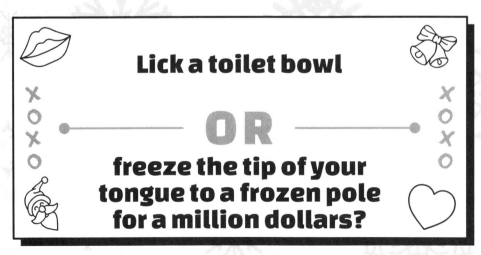

Lick a toilet bowl

OR

freeze the tip of your tongue to a frozen pole for a million dollars?

WOULD YOU RATHER?

Paint the inside of your house while nude

OR

mow the lawn wearing your partner's clothes?

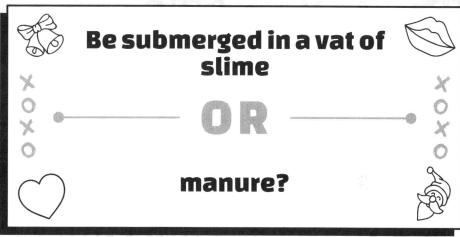

Be submerged in a vat of slime

OR

manure?

Eat your partner's boogers

OR

wear their used underwear?

WOULD YOU RATHER?

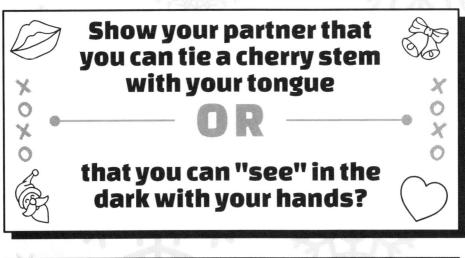

Show your partner that you can tie a cherry stem with your tongue

OR

that you can "see" in the dark with your hands?

Be blindfolded

OR

tied up during foreplay?

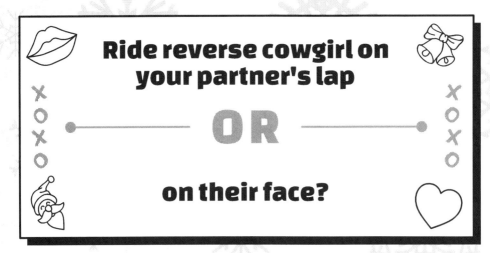

Ride reverse cowgirl on your partner's lap

OR

on their face?

WOULD YOU RATHER?

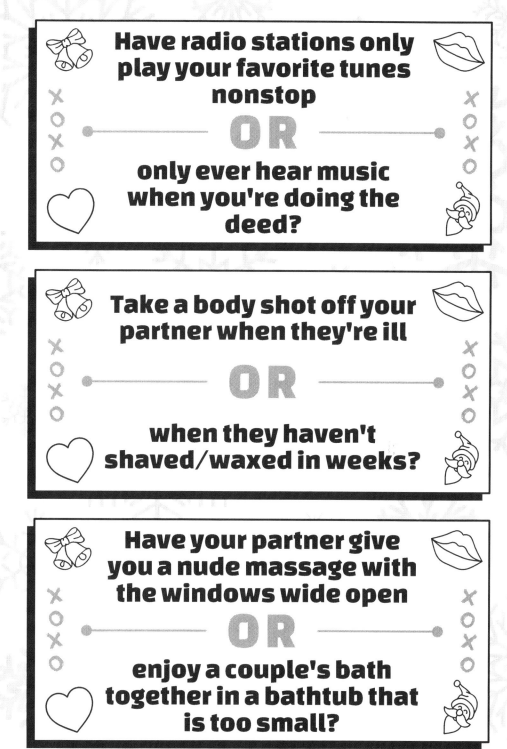

Have radio stations only play your favorite tunes nonstop

OR

only ever hear music when you're doing the deed?

Take a body shot off your partner when they're ill

OR

when they haven't shaved/waxed in weeks?

Have your partner give you a nude massage with the windows wide open

OR

enjoy a couple's bath together in a bathtub that is too small?

WOULD YOU RATHER?

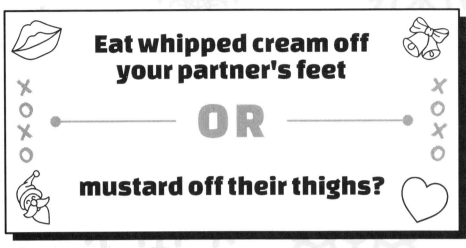

Eat whipped cream off your partner's feet

OR

mustard off their thighs?

Be about to "finish" and look up to see your dog staring at you

OR

hear your cat about to vomit while you're getting to the good part?

Toss a freshly cooked meal

OR

all your work assignments off the table to have sex?

WOULD YOU RATHER?

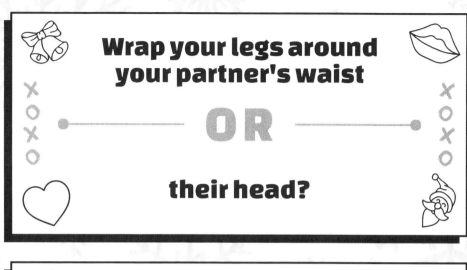

Wrap your legs around your partner's waist

OR

their head?

Attempt to have sex in the shower and fail

OR

do it on the beach successfully but get sand everywhere?

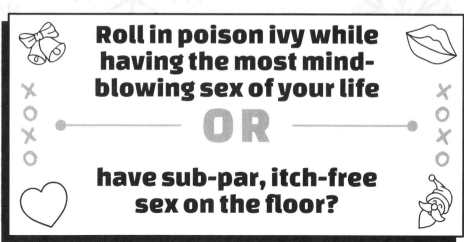

Roll in poison ivy while having the most mind-blowing sex of your life

OR

have sub-par, itch-free sex on the floor?

WOULD YOU RATHER?

Douse your body with hand sanitizer

OR

ketchup before getting down and dirty?

Wear a rubber

OR

woolen suit with holes cut out only for your naughty bits and your head?

Be "left on read" after a great night with your lover

OR

have them show up at your workplace with an embarrassingly large bouquet of flowers?

WOULD YOU RATHER?

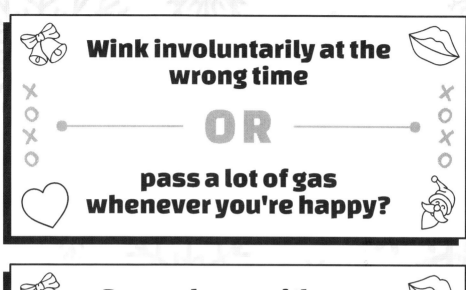

Wink involuntarily at the wrong time

OR

pass a lot of gas whenever you're happy?

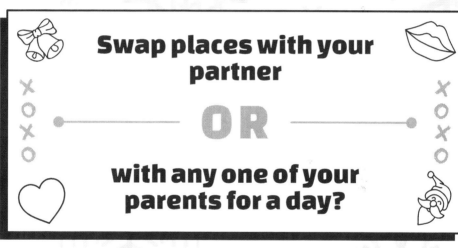

Swap places with your partner

OR

with any one of your parents for a day?

Become a ghost that can only haunt your exes

OR

a cat that constantly licks itself?

WOULD YOU RATHER?

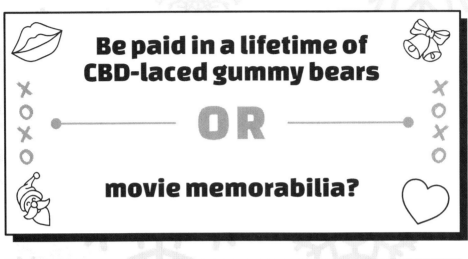

Be paid in a lifetime of CBD-laced gummy bears

OR

movie memorabilia?

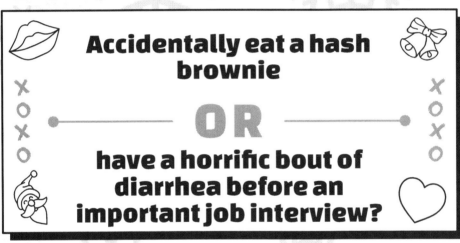

Accidentally eat a hash brownie

OR

have a horrific bout of diarrhea before an important job interview?

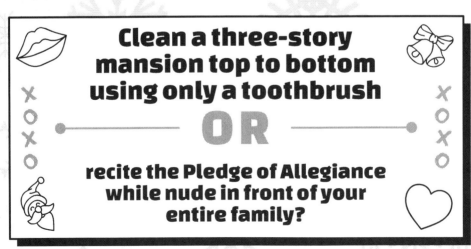

Clean a three-story mansion top to bottom using only a toothbrush

OR

recite the Pledge of Allegiance while nude in front of your entire family?

WOULD YOU RATHER?

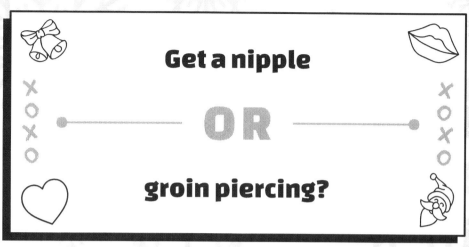

Get a nipple

OR

groin piercing?

Have your waitress use their mouth

OR

armpit to open your bottle of alcohol at a fancy restaurant?

Have a hot boss who wears attractive clothes to work every day

OR

a dowdy-looking boss who constantly hits on you at work?

WOULD YOU RATHER?

Drive 700 miles to get laid

OR

have one of your parents pick and approve of each of your potential partners?

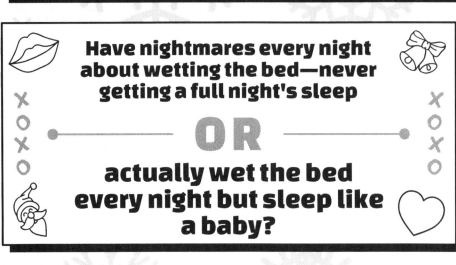

Have nightmares every night about wetting the bed—never getting a full night's sleep

OR

actually wet the bed every night but sleep like a baby?

Eat yellow snow

OR

smell like your own farts for the rest of your life for a million dollars?

WOULD YOU RATHER?

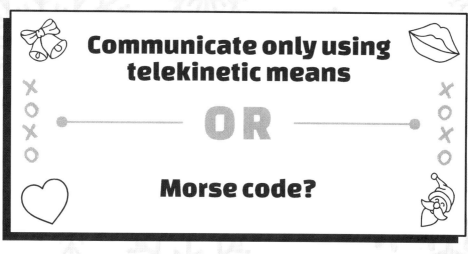

Communicate only using telekinetic means

OR

Morse code?

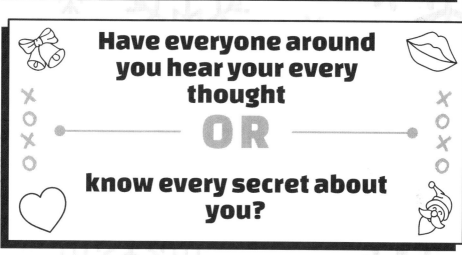

Have everyone around you hear your every thought

OR

know every secret about you?

Worship your cat

OR

pick every flea off your dog by hand?

WOULD YOU RATHER?

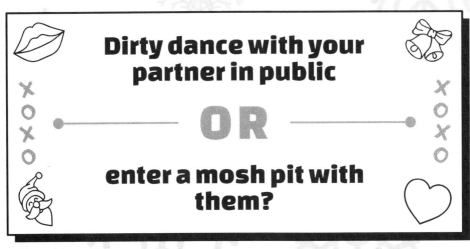

Dirty dance with your partner in public

OR

enter a mosh pit with them?

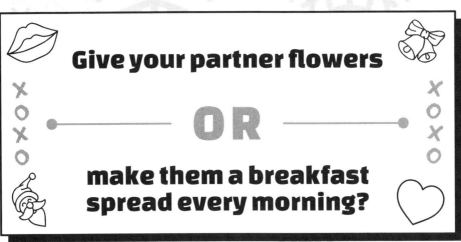

Give your partner flowers

OR

make them a breakfast spread every morning?

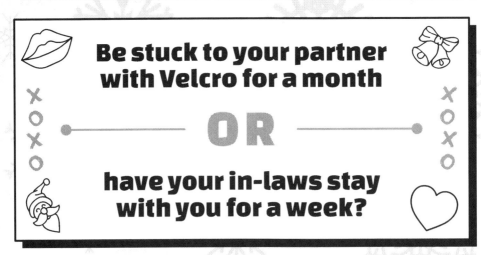

Be stuck to your partner with Velcro for a month

OR

have your in-laws stay with you for a week?

WOULD YOU RATHER?

Never change your underwear

OR

your socks?

Shave your head and eyebrows

OR

never be allowed to bathe again?

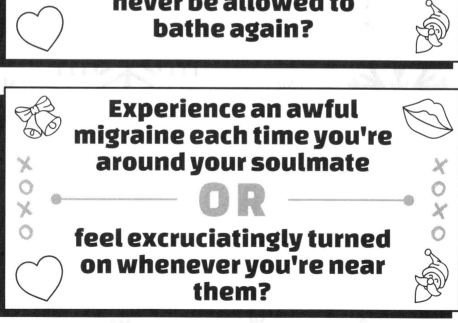

Experience an awful migraine each time you're around your soulmate

OR

feel excruciatingly turned on whenever you're near them?

WOULD YOU RATHER?

Use your words

OR

your hands to initiate foreplay?

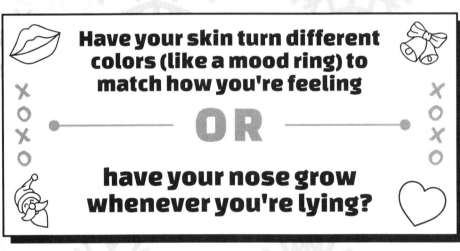

Have your skin turn different colors (like a mood ring) to match how you're feeling

OR

have your nose grow whenever you're lying?

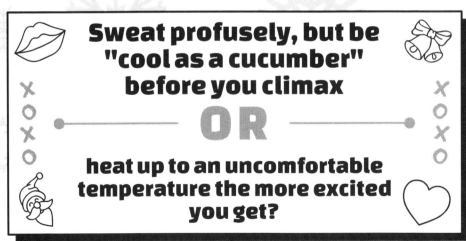

Sweat profusely, but be "cool as a cucumber" before you climax

OR

heat up to an uncomfortable temperature the more excited you get?

WOULD YOU RATHER?

Feel like you're melting whenever your soulmate touches you

OR

feel like your whole body is being electrified?

Have superhuman strength to carry your partner around

OR

have an astounding amount of flexibility to contort yourself in any way you wish?

Be insanely attractive

OR

unquestionably intelligent?

WOULD YOU RATHER?

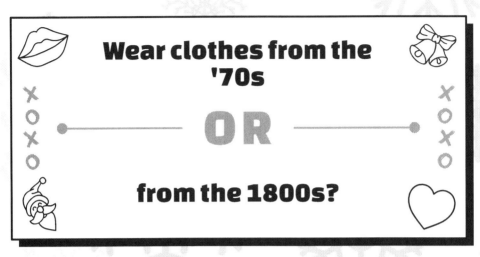

Wear clothes from the '70s

OR

from the 1800s?

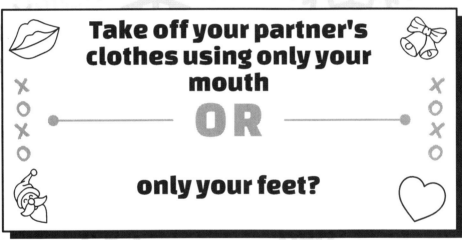

Take off your partner's clothes using only your mouth

OR

only your feet?

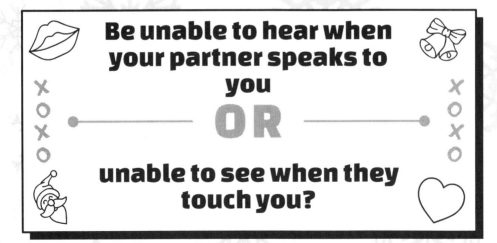

Be unable to hear when your partner speaks to you

OR

unable to see when they touch you?

WOULD YOU RATHER?

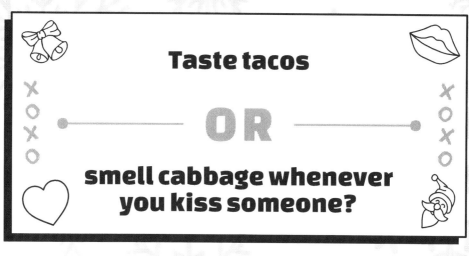

Taste tacos

OR

smell cabbage whenever you kiss someone?

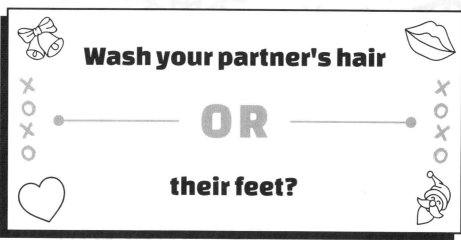

Wash your partner's hair

OR

their feet?

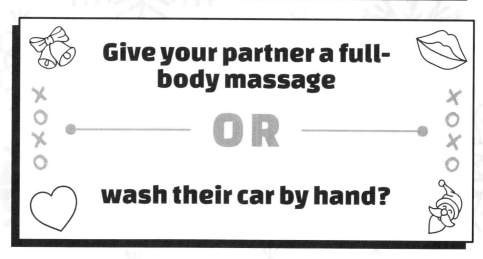

Give your partner a full-body massage

OR

wash their car by hand?

WOULD YOU RATHER?

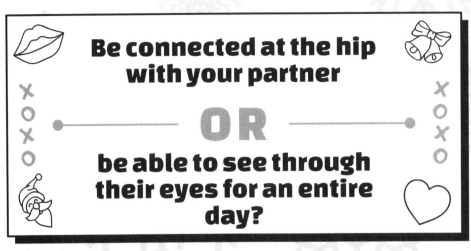

Be connected at the hip with your partner

OR

be able to see through their eyes for an entire day?

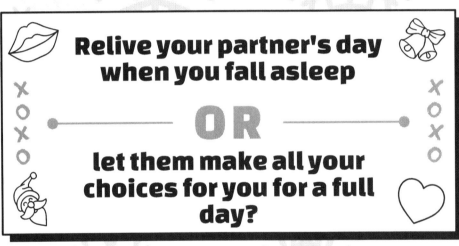

Relive your partner's day when you fall asleep

OR

let them make all your choices for you for a full day?

Eat a meal prepared by your partner

OR

your partner's parents?

WOULD YOU RATHER?

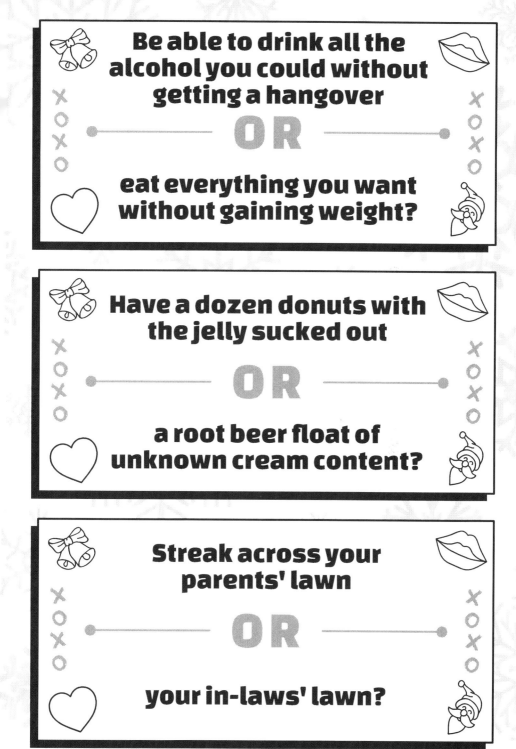

Be able to drink all the alcohol you could without getting a hangover

OR

eat everything you want without gaining weight?

Have a dozen donuts with the jelly sucked out

OR

a root beer float of unknown cream content?

Streak across your parents' lawn

OR

your in-laws' lawn?

WOULD YOU RATHER?

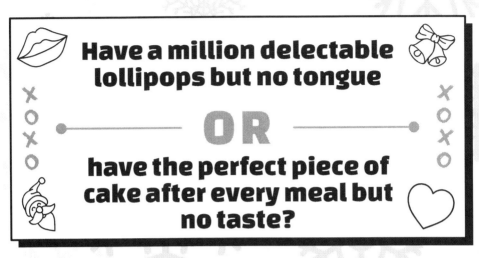

Have a million delectable lollipops but no tongue

OR

have the perfect piece of cake after every meal but no taste?

Wear edible underwear

OR

tear-away clothing for a sexy session with your partner?

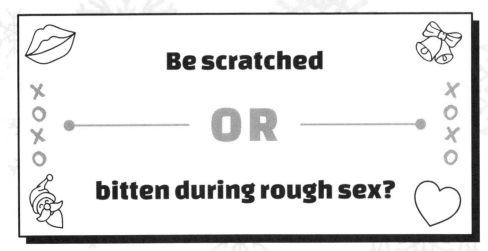

Be scratched

OR

bitten during rough sex?

WOULD YOU RATHER?

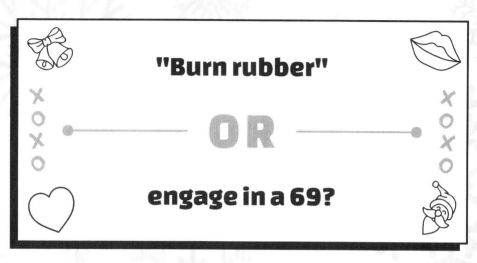

"Burn rubber"

OR

engage in a 69?

Have your partner role play

OR

get straight down to business?

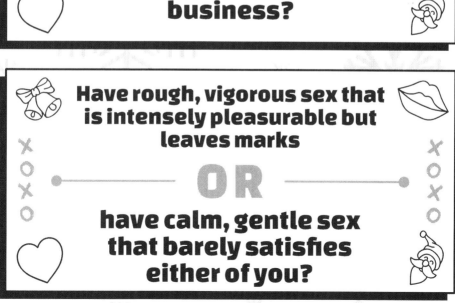

Have rough, vigorous sex that is intensely pleasurable but leaves marks

OR

have calm, gentle sex that barely satisfies either of you?

WOULD YOU RATHER?

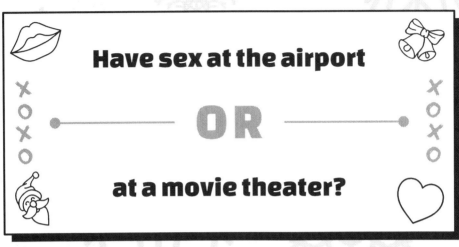

Have sex at the airport

OR

at a movie theater?

"Tank up" on alcohol that never gets you drunk

OR

your partner's climax fluid that is quite intoxicating?

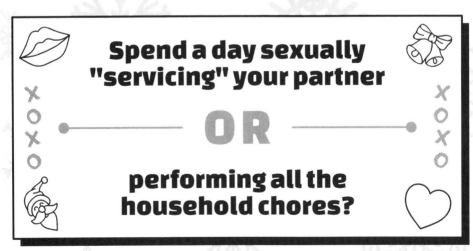

Spend a day sexually "servicing" your partner

OR

performing all the household chores?

WOULD YOU RATHER?

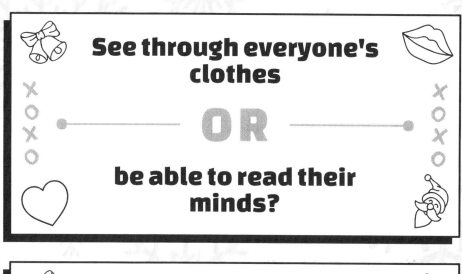

See through everyone's clothes

OR

be able to read their minds?

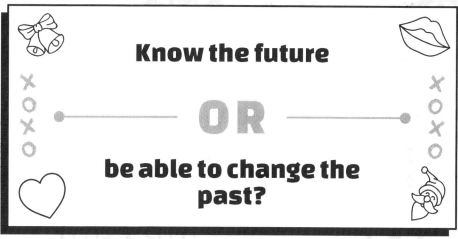

Know the future

OR

be able to change the past?

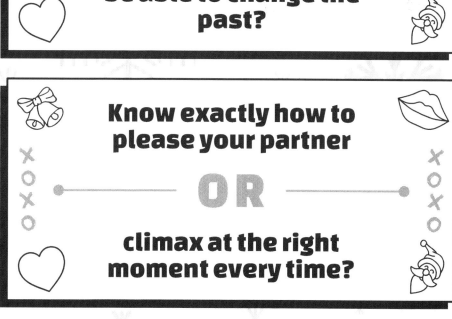

Know exactly how to please your partner

OR

climax at the right moment every time?

WOULD YOU RATHER?

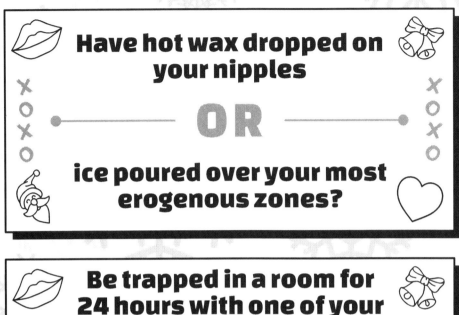

Have hot wax dropped on your nipples

OR

ice poured over your most erogenous zones?

Be trapped in a room for 24 hours with one of your in-laws

OR

your ex?

Make a million dollars doing something against your morals

OR

a thousand dollars doing something you love?

WOULD YOU RATHER?

Speak with a French accent and be a terrible chef

OR

an Italian accent but be a horrible lover?

Have stripes

OR

spots covering your entire body?

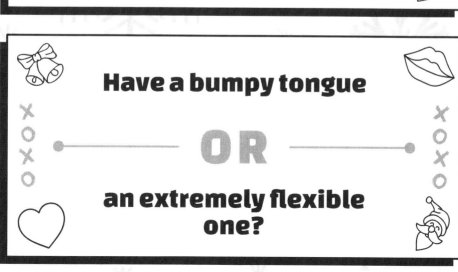

Have a bumpy tongue

OR

an extremely flexible one?

WOULD YOU RATHER?

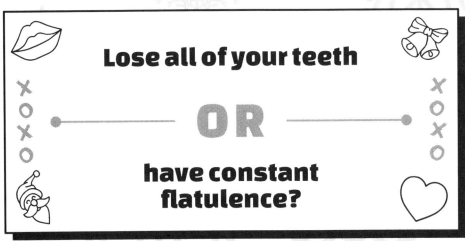

Lose all of your teeth

OR

have constant flatulence?

Have to lick every family member's dirty dinner plate

OR

your dog's food dish clean?

Get a professional painting of your partner's genitals

OR

a $50 gift card for Valentine's Day?

WOULD YOU RATHER?

Have to agree to not have sex with someone you're really attracted to for a year

OR

have sex with someone you find unattractive every night?

Have bright red nose hair

OR

have black nose hair that never stops growing?

Accidentally send a sexy email to your boss

OR

have a coworker overhear you talking dirty on your lunch break?

WOULD YOU RATHER?

Drink a gallon of milk on a dare

OR

divulge your most damning secret?

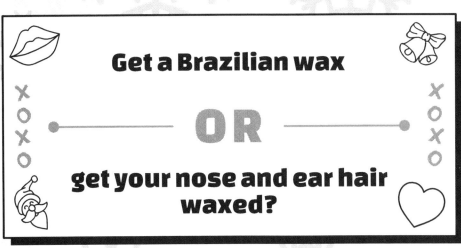

Get a Brazilian wax

OR

get your nose and ear hair waxed?

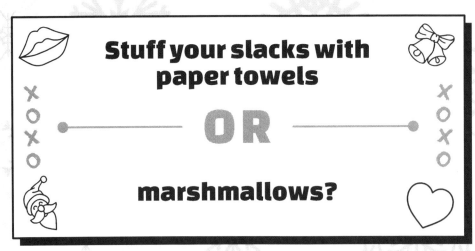

Stuff your slacks with paper towels

OR

marshmallows?

WOULD YOU RATHER?

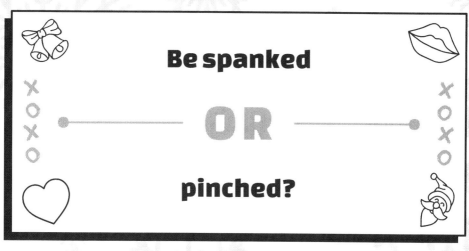

Be spanked

OR

pinched?

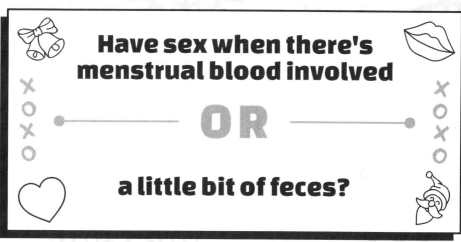

Have sex when there's menstrual blood involved

OR

a little bit of feces?

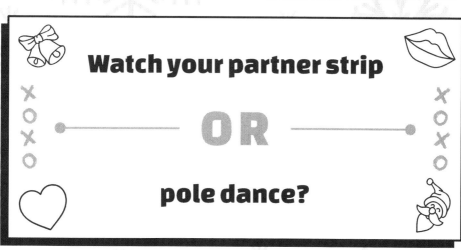

Watch your partner strip

OR

pole dance?

WOULD YOU RATHER?

Eat a small bowl of your own fingernail clippings

OR

a handful of your partner's boogers?

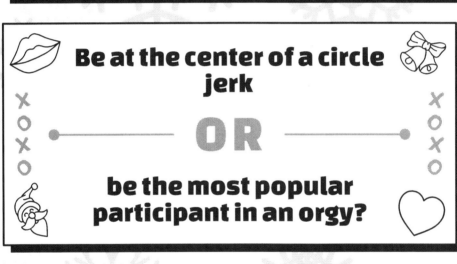

Be at the center of a circle jerk

OR

be the most popular participant in an orgy?

Have someone polish your "family jewels" by hand

OR

via spit-shine?

WOULD YOU RATHER?

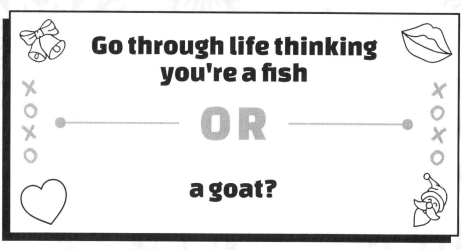

Go through life thinking you're a fish

OR

a goat?

Let your partner have unfettered access to your phone

OR

let them choose your next tattoo to be completed by them personally?

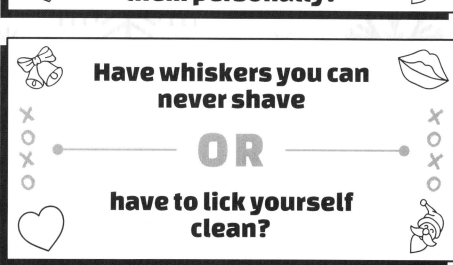

Have whiskers you can never shave

OR

have to lick yourself clean?

WOULD YOU RATHER?

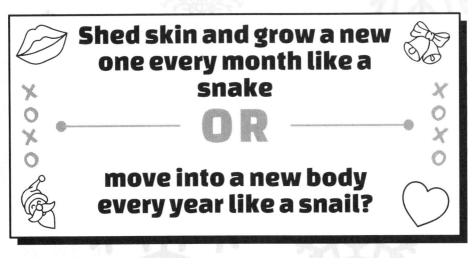

Shed skin and grow a new one every month like a snake

OR

move into a new body every year like a snail?

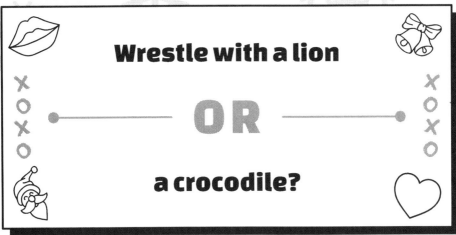

Wrestle with a lion

OR

a crocodile?

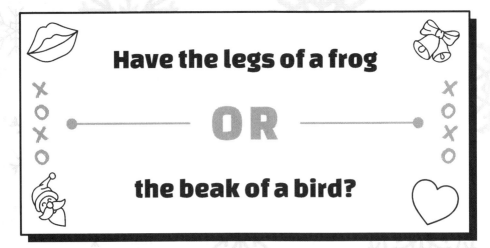

Have the legs of a frog

OR

the beak of a bird?

WOULD YOU RATHER?

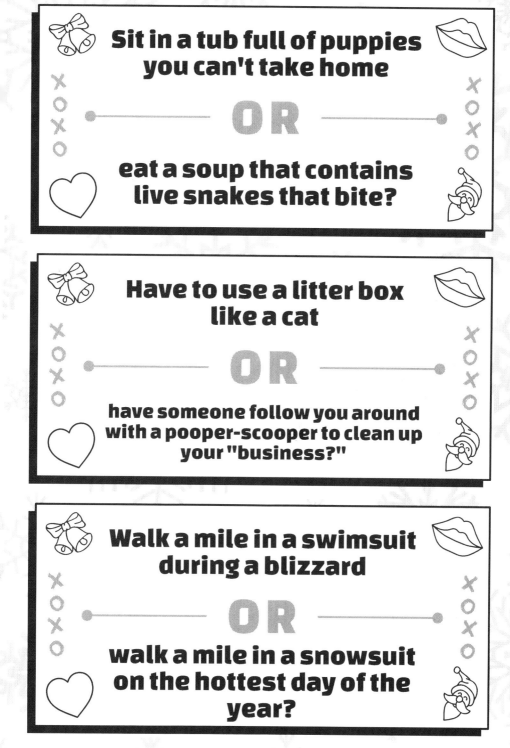

Sit in a tub full of puppies you can't take home

OR

eat a soup that contains live snakes that bite?

Have to use a litter box like a cat

OR

have someone follow you around with a pooper-scooper to clean up your "business?"

Walk a mile in a swimsuit during a blizzard

OR

walk a mile in a snowsuit on the hottest day of the year?

WOULD YOU RATHER?

Star in a sex tape with your partner

OR

watch porn together with them?

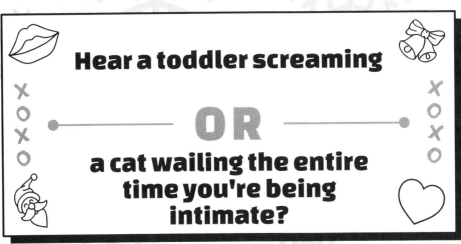

Hear a toddler screaming

OR

a cat wailing the entire time you're being intimate?

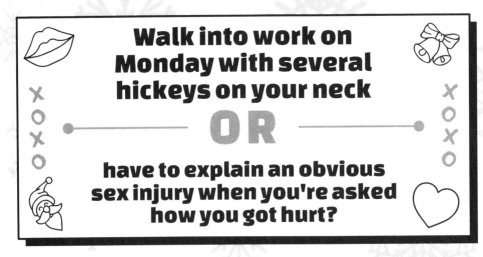

Walk into work on Monday with several hickeys on your neck

OR

have to explain an obvious sex injury when you're asked how you got hurt?

WOULD YOU RATHER?

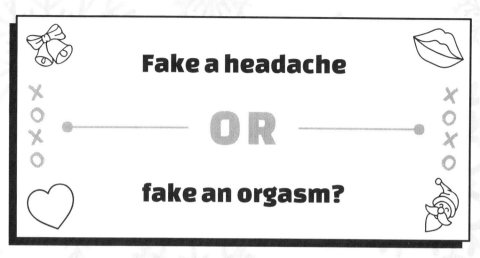

Fake a headache

OR

fake an orgasm?

Always be thirsty

OR

always be horny?

Never wear underwear

OR

always have to wear nipple clamps?

WOULD YOU RATHER?

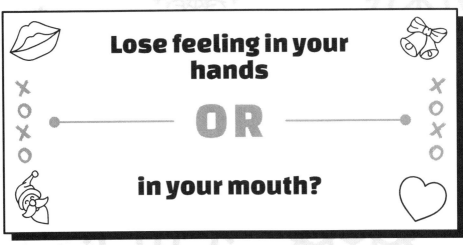

Lose feeling in your hands

OR

in your mouth?

Have everything you put in your mouth taste like chicken

OR

be able to taste your partner's genitals every time you eat chicken?

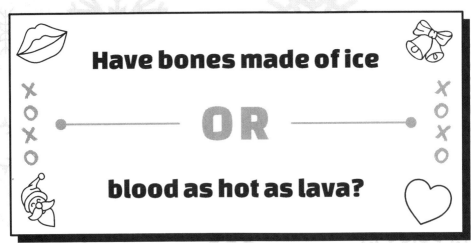

Have bones made of ice

OR

blood as hot as lava?

WOULD YOU RATHER?

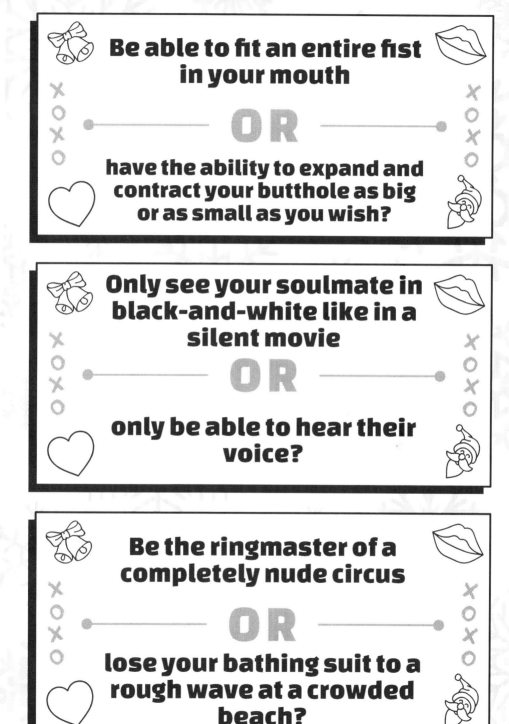

Be able to fit an entire fist in your mouth

OR

have the ability to expand and contract your butthole as big or as small as you wish?

Only see your soulmate in black-and-white like in a silent movie

OR

only be able to hear their voice?

Be the ringmaster of a completely nude circus

OR

lose your bathing suit to a rough wave at a crowded beach?

WOULD YOU RATHER?

Wear underwear made by your grandmother

OR

made out of starfish?

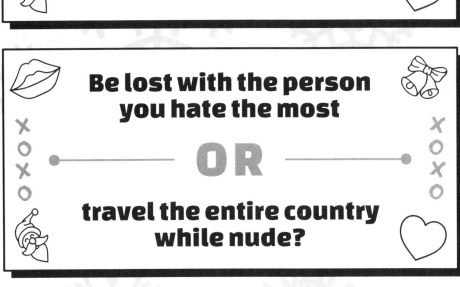

Be lost with the person you hate the most

OR

travel the entire country while nude?

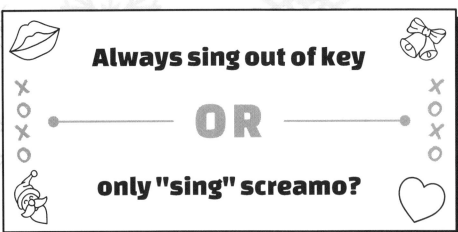

Always sing out of key

OR

only "sing" screamo?

WOULD YOU RATHER?

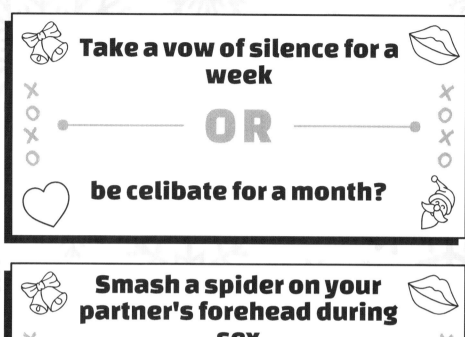

Take a vow of silence for a week

OR

be celibate for a month?

Smash a spider on your partner's forehead during sex

OR

have a parrot on their shoulder watching the whole time?

Let your partner use rusty scissors to cut your fingernails

OR

drink every last sip of leftover beer in the bottles at your favorite bar?

WOULD YOU RATHER?

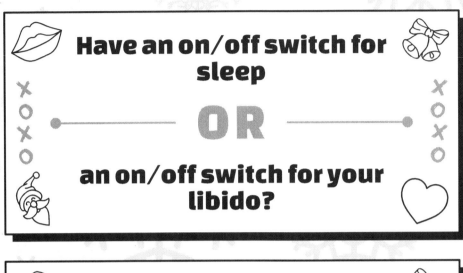

Have an on/off switch for sleep

OR

an on/off switch for your libido?

Be publicly ranked by your ex-lovers

OR

have your accurate height and weight published for all to see?

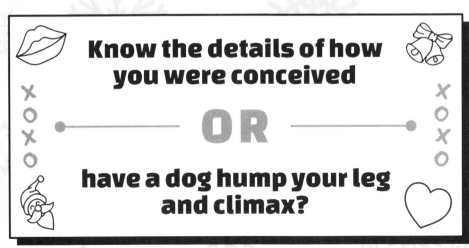

Know the details of how you were conceived

OR

have a dog hump your leg and climax?

WOULD YOU RATHER?

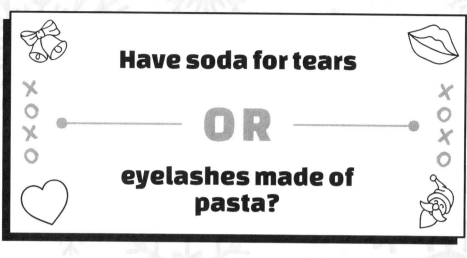

Have soda for tears

OR

eyelashes made of pasta?

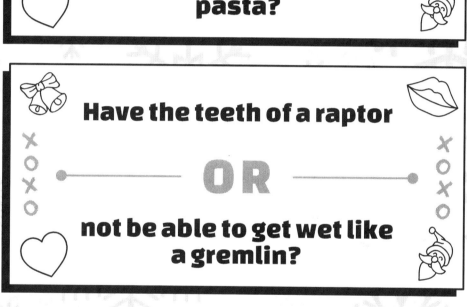

Have the teeth of a raptor

OR

not be able to get wet like a gremlin?

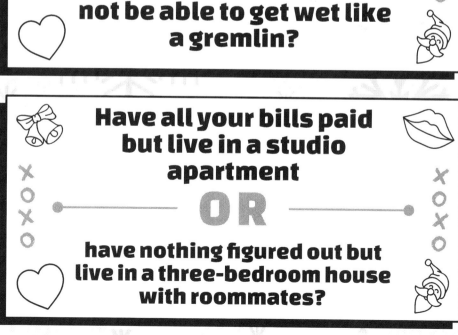

Have all your bills paid but live in a studio apartment

OR

have nothing figured out but live in a three-bedroom house with roommates?

WOULD YOU RATHER?

Have roommates that smoke marijuana day and night

OR

roommates that drink and party excessively?

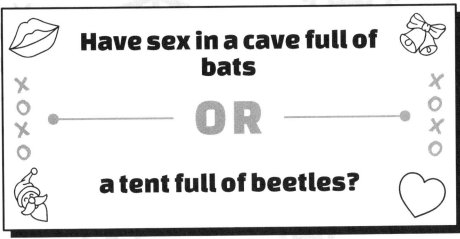

Have sex in a cave full of bats

OR

a tent full of beetles?

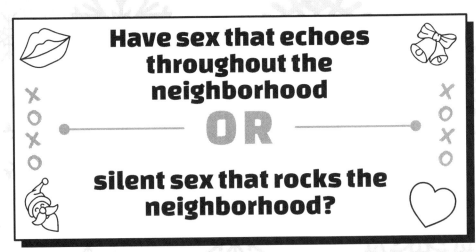

Have sex that echoes throughout the neighborhood

OR

silent sex that rocks the neighborhood?

WOULD YOU RATHER?

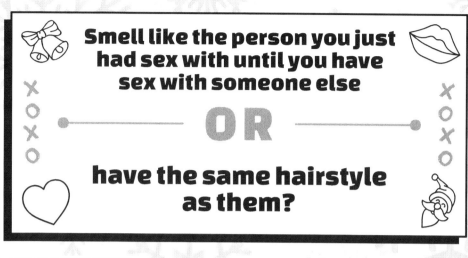

Smell like the person you just had sex with until you have sex with someone else

OR

have the same hairstyle as them?

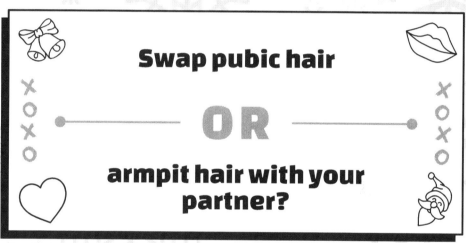

Swap pubic hair

OR

armpit hair with your partner?

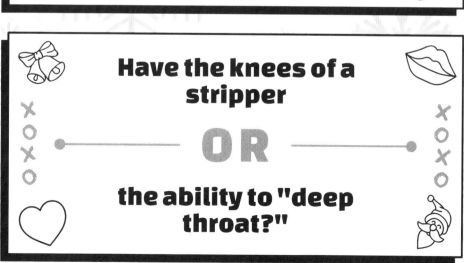

Have the knees of a stripper

OR

the ability to "deep throat?"

WOULD YOU RATHER?

Have a foot fetish

OR

be into BDSM?

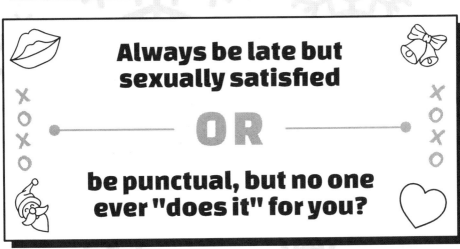

Always be late but sexually satisfied

OR

be punctual, but no one ever "does it" for you?

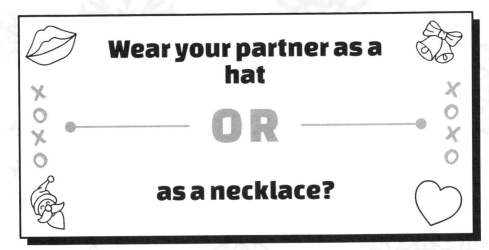

Wear your partner as a hat

OR

as a necklace?

WOULD YOU RATHER?

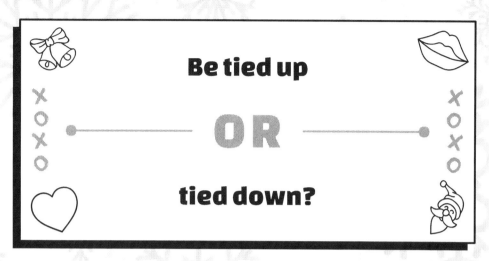

Be tied up

OR

tied down?

Have your partner
handcuff you

OR

flog you?

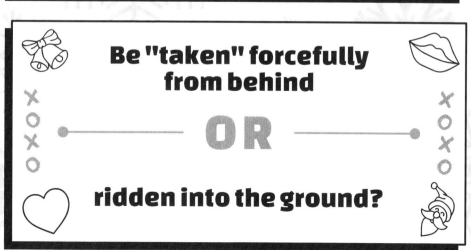

Be "taken" forcefully
from behind

OR

ridden into the ground?

WOULD YOU RATHER?

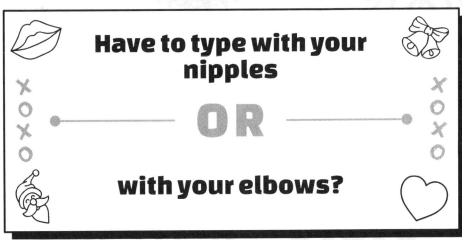

Have to type with your nipples

OR

with your elbows?

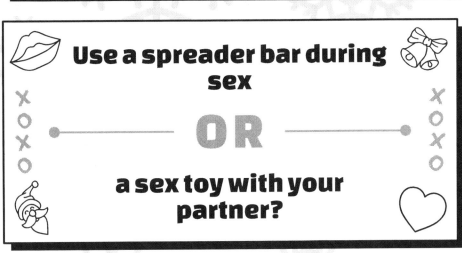

Use a spreader bar during sex

OR

a sex toy with your partner?

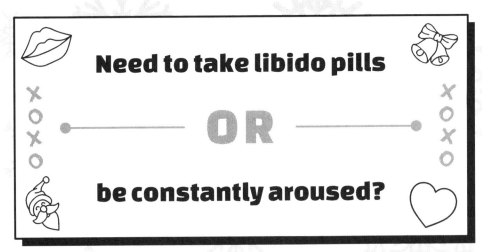

Need to take libido pills

OR

be constantly aroused?

WOULD YOU RATHER?

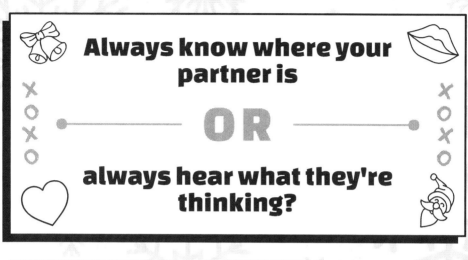

Always know where your partner is

OR

always hear what they're thinking?

Read every book your partner has read

OR

watch every TV show they've watched?

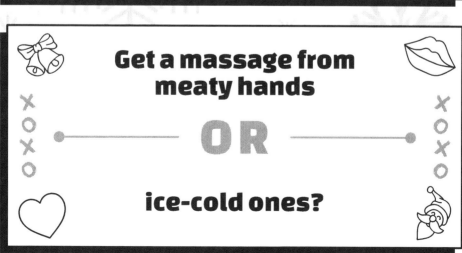

Get a massage from meaty hands

OR

ice-cold ones?

WOULD YOU RATHER?

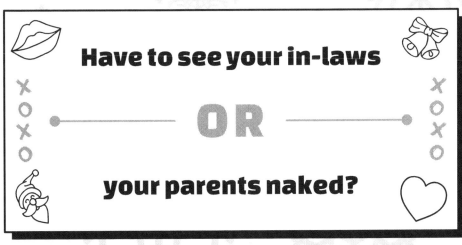

Have to see your in-laws

OR

your parents naked?

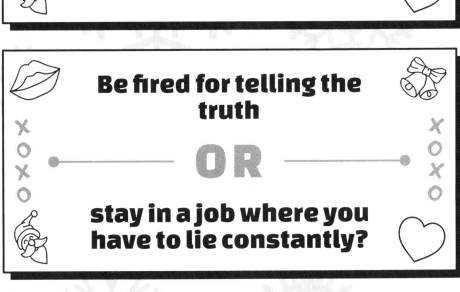

Be fired for telling the truth

OR

stay in a job where you have to lie constantly?

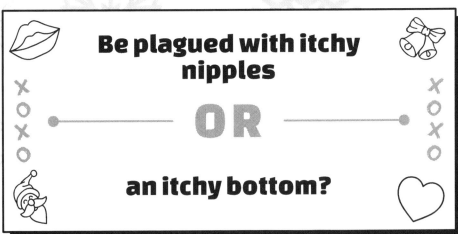

Be plagued with itchy nipples

OR

an itchy bottom?

WOULD YOU RATHER?

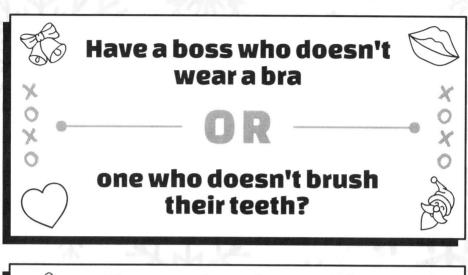

Have a boss who doesn't wear a bra

OR

one who doesn't brush their teeth?

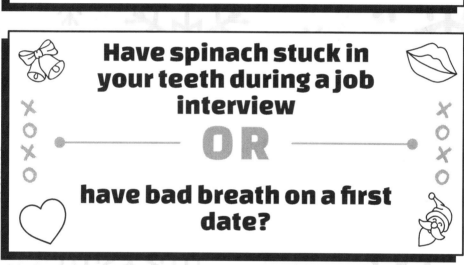

Have spinach stuck in your teeth during a job interview

OR

have bad breath on a first date?

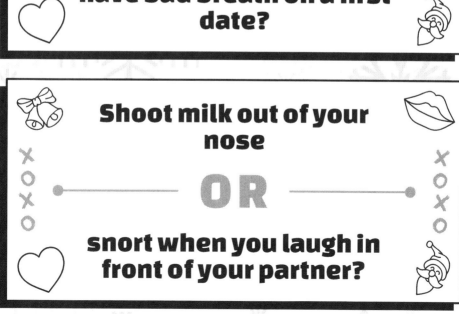

Shoot milk out of your nose

OR

snort when you laugh in front of your partner?

WOULD YOU RATHER?

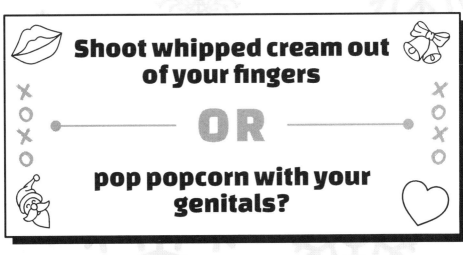

Shoot whipped cream out of your fingers

OR

pop popcorn with your genitals?

Always look like you have makeup on

OR

never have to brush your hair?

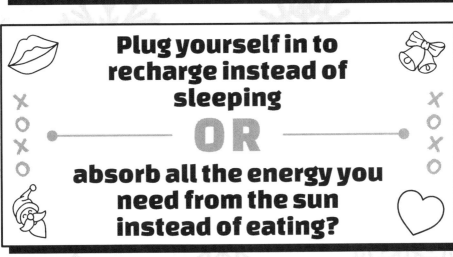

Plug yourself in to recharge instead of sleeping

OR

absorb all the energy you need from the sun instead of eating?

WOULD YOU RATHER?

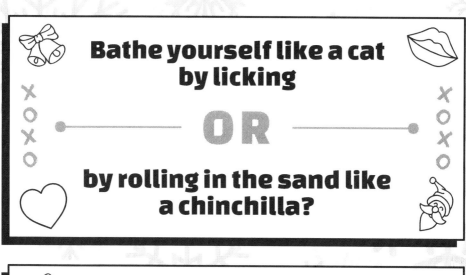

Bathe yourself like a cat by licking

OR

by rolling in the sand like a chinchilla?

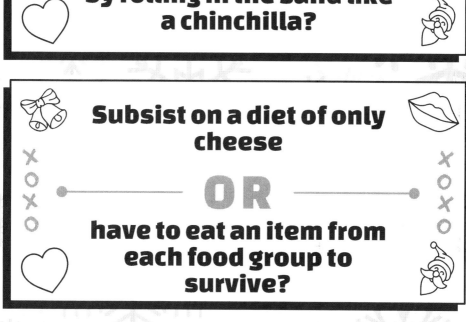

Subsist on a diet of only cheese

OR

have to eat an item from each food group to survive?

Spell everything you write perfectly

OR

misspeak every time you try to talk?

WOULD YOU RATHER?

Laugh when the joke isn't funny

OR

tell your friend that they "look good" when they really don't?

Your partner have platonic friends of the opposite sex

OR

still be "good friends" with their ex?

Go ghost-hunting

OR

have your palm read?

WOULD YOU RATHER?

Be a model

OR

an Olympic gold medalist?

Live next door to a garbage dump

OR

a loud highway?

Watch paint dry

OR

hair grow?

WOULD YOU RATHER?

Arrive to work in a garbage truck

OR

after riding a bicycle the whole way?

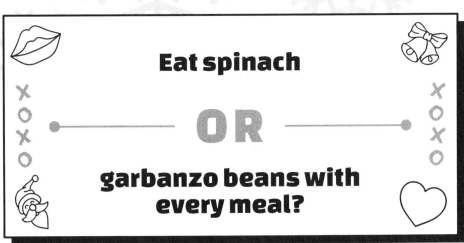

Eat spinach

OR

garbanzo beans with every meal?

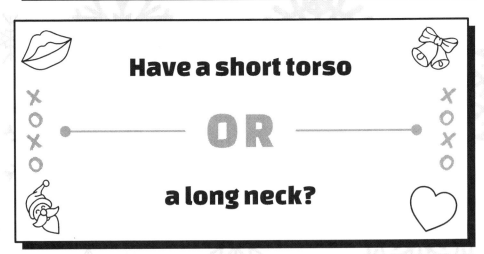

Have a short torso

OR

a long neck?

WOULD YOU RATHER?

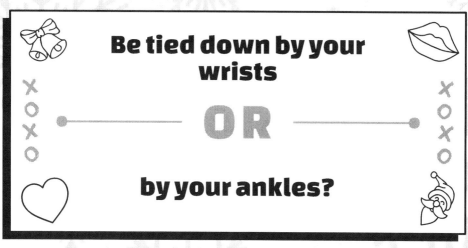

Be tied down by your wrists

OR

by your ankles?

Role-play with your partner wearing a uniform

OR

wearing lingerie?

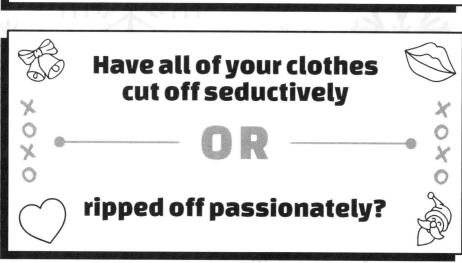

Have all of your clothes cut off seductively

OR

ripped off passionately?

WOULD YOU RATHER?

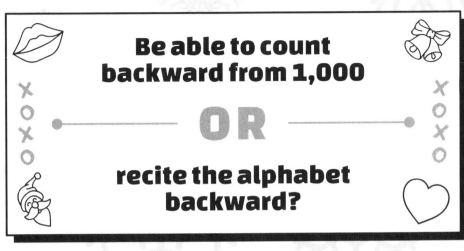

Be able to count backward from 1,000

OR

recite the alphabet backward?

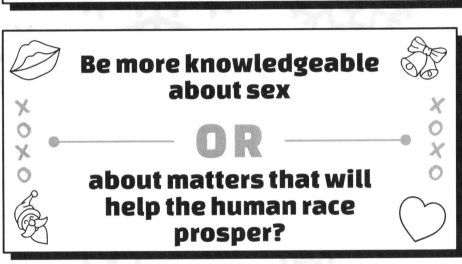

Be more knowledgeable about sex

OR

about matters that will help the human race prosper?

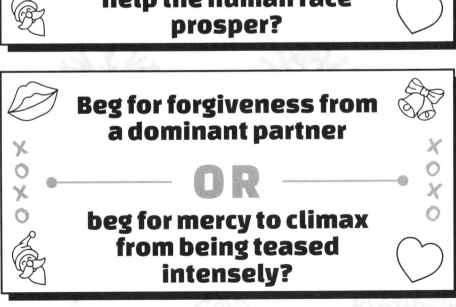

Beg for forgiveness from a dominant partner

OR

beg for mercy to climax from being teased intensely?

WOULD YOU RATHER?

Have an "afternoon delight"

OR

a "midnight snack?"

Share a blanket

OR

a pillow with your partner?

Accidentally drink sour milk

OR

squish a slug between your toes?

WOULD YOU RATHER?

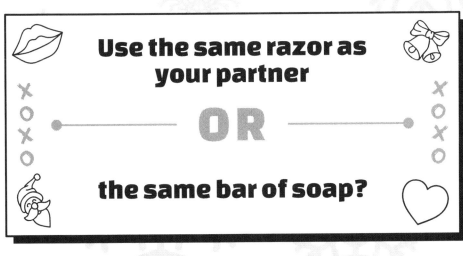

Use the same razor as your partner

OR

the same bar of soap?

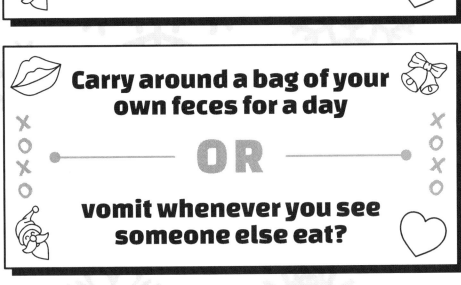

Carry around a bag of your own feces for a day

OR

vomit whenever you see someone else eat?

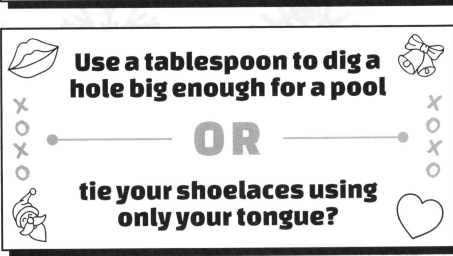

Use a tablespoon to dig a hole big enough for a pool

OR

tie your shoelaces using only your tongue?

WOULD YOU RATHER?

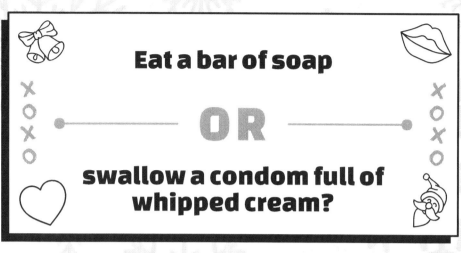

Eat a bar of soap

OR

swallow a condom full of whipped cream?

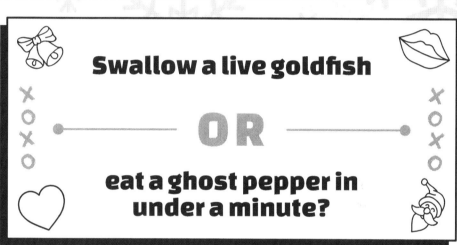

Swallow a live goldfish

OR

eat a ghost pepper in under a minute?

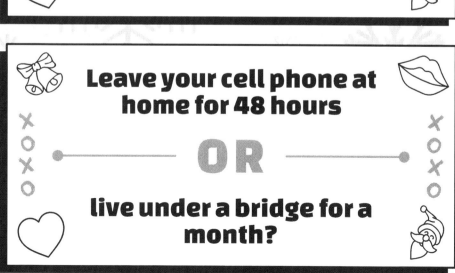

Leave your cell phone at home for 48 hours

OR

live under a bridge for a month?

WOULD YOU RATHER?

Wear the same underwear

OR

a bathing suit instead of underwear for a month?

Have your partner grab your thighs

OR

your butt to pull you closer?

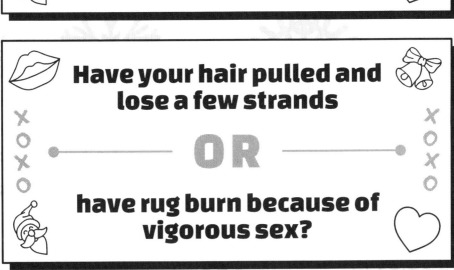

Have your hair pulled and lose a few strands

OR

have rug burn because of vigorous sex?

WOULD YOU RATHER?

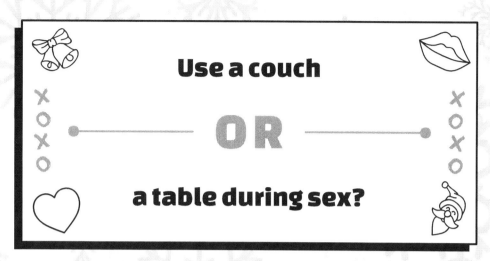

Use a couch

OR

a table during sex?

Your partner sound like a porn star

OR

look like one?

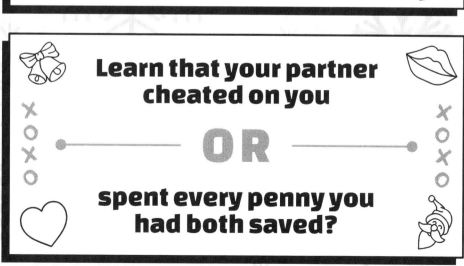

Learn that your partner cheated on you

OR

spent every penny you had both saved?

WOULD YOU RATHER?

Receive a bouquet of "I'm sorry" flowers

OR

a hand-written apology letter?

Feel drunk

OR

feel forever thirsty when you're in love?

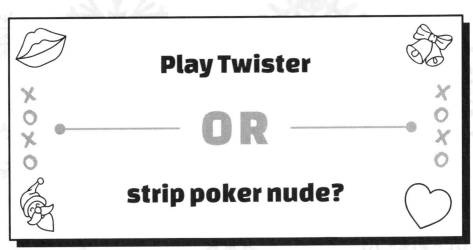

Play Twister

OR

strip poker nude?

WOULD YOU RATHER?

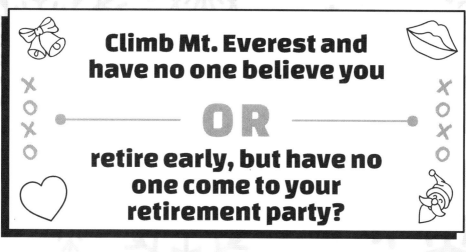

Climb Mt. Everest and have no one believe you

OR

retire early, but have no one come to your retirement party?

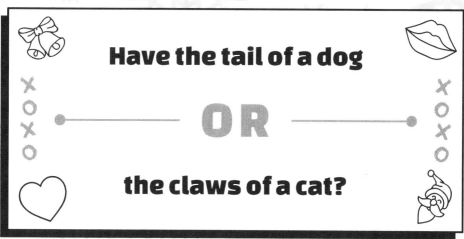

Have the tail of a dog

OR

the claws of a cat?

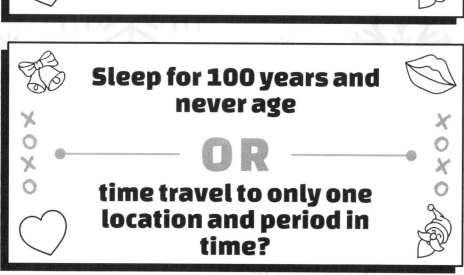

Sleep for 100 years and never age

OR

time travel to only one location and period in time?

WOULD YOU RATHER?

Work from home and be the most beautiful, put-together version of yourself

OR

go to work every weekday as the tired, hot-mess version of yourself but have the best coworkers?

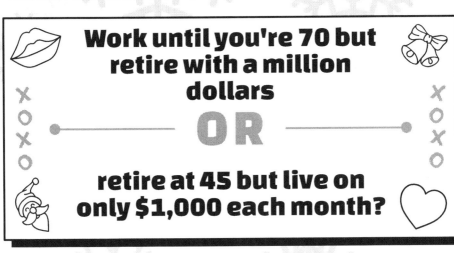

Work until you're 70 but retire with a million dollars

OR

retire at 45 but live on only $1,000 each month?

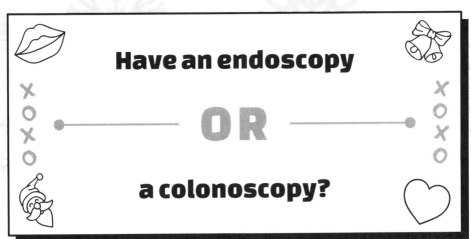

Have an endoscopy

OR

a colonoscopy?

WOULD YOU RATHER?

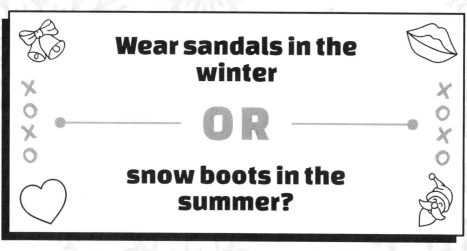

Wear sandals in the winter

OR

snow boots in the summer?

Have rain every day but a warm fire indoors

OR

sunny weather every day but no air conditioning?

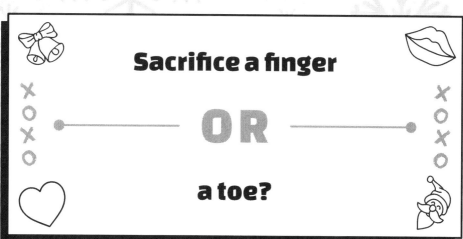

Sacrifice a finger

OR

a toe?

WOULD YOU RATHER?

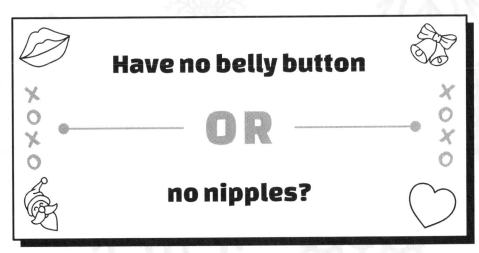

Have no belly button

OR

no nipples?

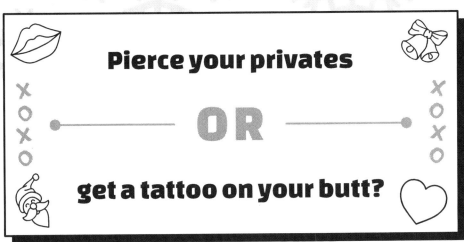

Pierce your privates

OR

get a tattoo on your butt?

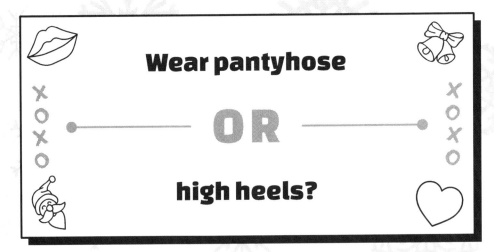

Wear pantyhose

OR

high heels?

WOULD YOU RATHER?

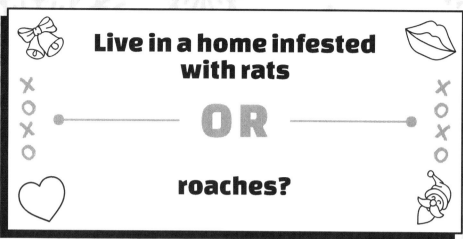

Live in a home infested with rats

OR

roaches?

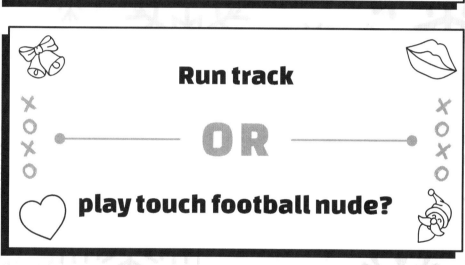

Run track

OR

play touch football nude?

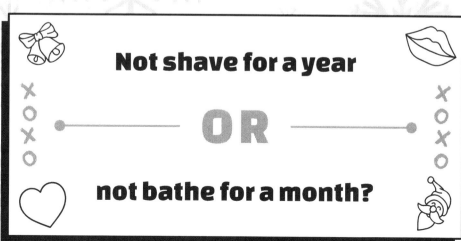

Not shave for a year

OR

not bathe for a month?

WOULD YOU RATHER?

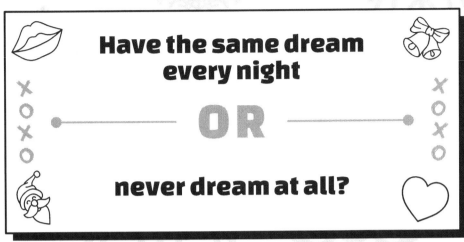

Have the same dream every night

OR

never dream at all?

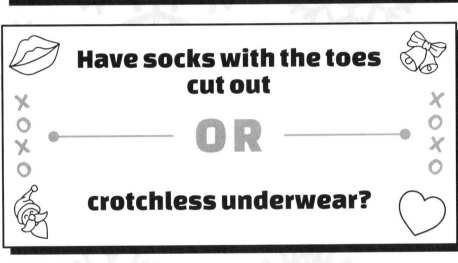

Have socks with the toes cut out

OR

crotchless underwear?

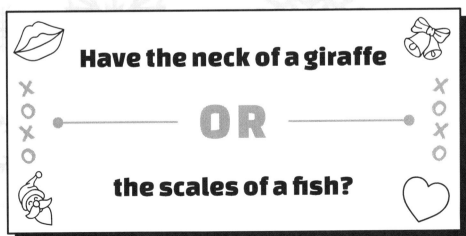

Have the neck of a giraffe

OR

the scales of a fish?

WOULD YOU RATHER?

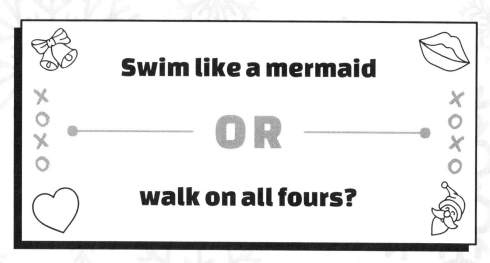

Swim like a mermaid

OR

walk on all fours?

Smell like a skunk

OR

compost?

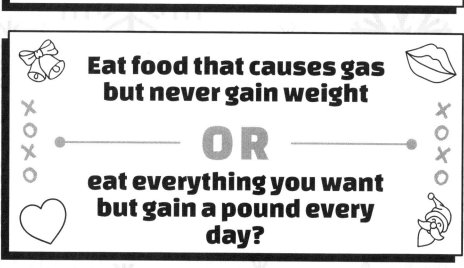

Eat food that causes gas but never gain weight

OR

eat everything you want but gain a pound every day?

WOULD YOU RATHER?

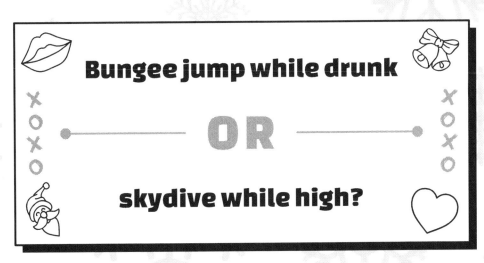

Bungee jump while drunk

OR

skydive while high?

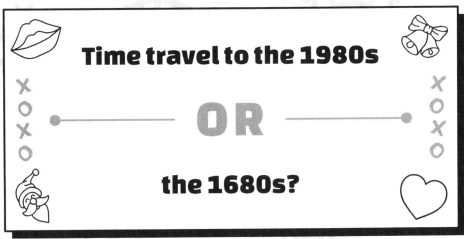

Time travel to the 1980s

OR

the 1680s?

Be immune to every disease

OR

cure cancer for everyone else?

WOULD YOU RATHER?

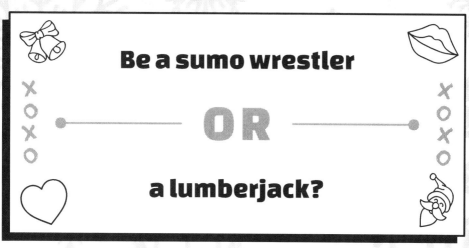

Be a sumo wrestler

OR

a lumberjack?

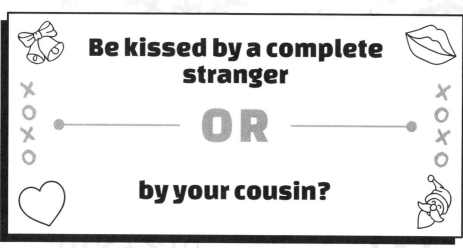

Be kissed by a complete stranger

OR

by your cousin?

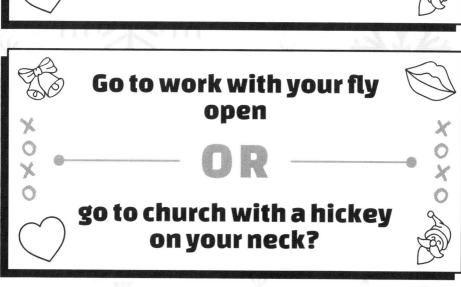

Go to work with your fly open

OR

go to church with a hickey on your neck?

WOULD YOU RATHER?

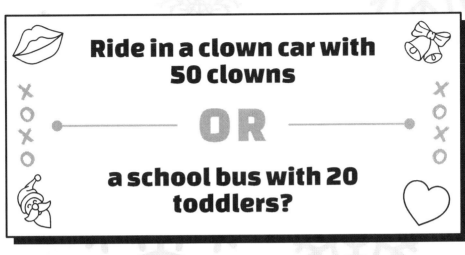

Ride in a clown car with 50 clowns

OR

a school bus with 20 toddlers?

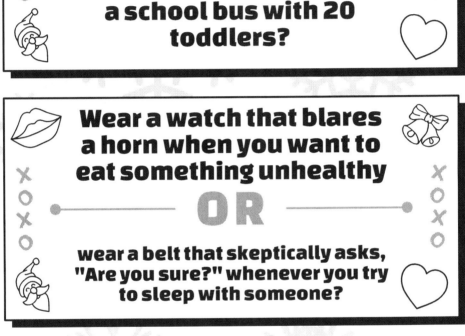

Wear a watch that blares a horn when you want to eat something unhealthy

OR

wear a belt that skeptically asks, "Are you sure?" whenever you try to sleep with someone?

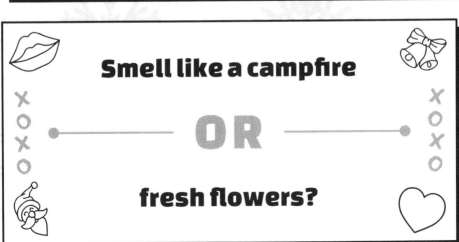

Smell like a campfire

OR

fresh flowers?

WOULD YOU RATHER?

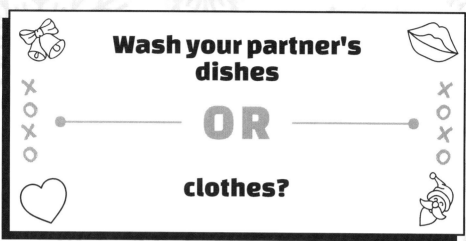

Wash your partner's dishes

OR

clothes?

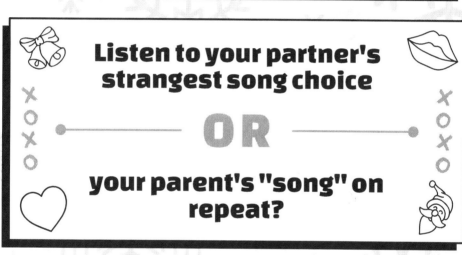

Listen to your partner's strangest song choice

OR

your parent's "song" on repeat?

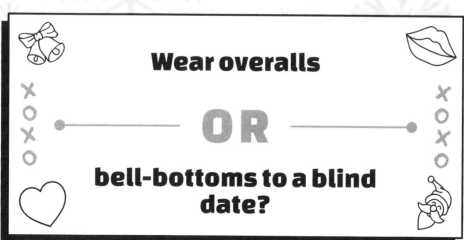

Wear overalls

OR

bell-bottoms to a blind date?

WOULD YOU RATHER?

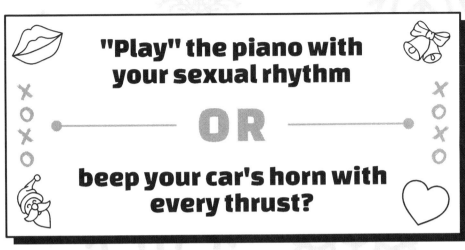

"Play" the piano with your sexual rhythm

OR

beep your car's horn with every thrust?

Have sex on your partner's libido schedule

OR

have them decide what dinner will be for a month?

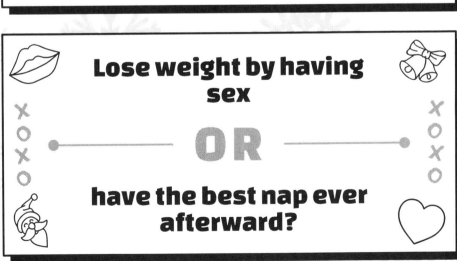

Lose weight by having sex

OR

have the best nap ever afterward?

WOULD YOU RATHER?

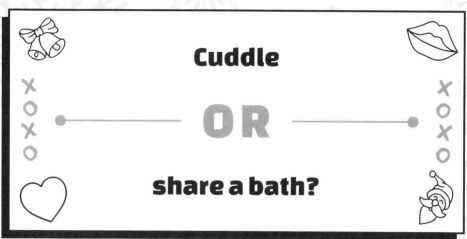

Cuddle

OR

share a bath?

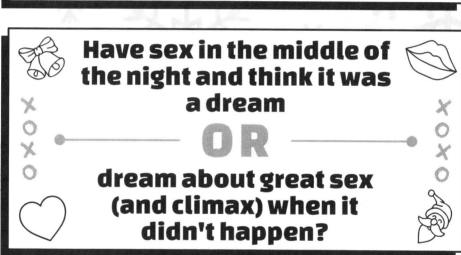

Have sex in the middle of the night and think it was a dream

OR

dream about great sex (and climax) when it didn't happen?

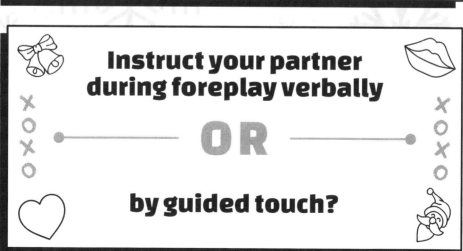

Instruct your partner during foreplay verbally

OR

by guided touch?

WOULD YOU RATHER?

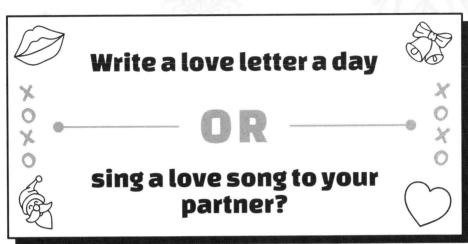

Write a love letter a day

OR

sing a love song to your partner?

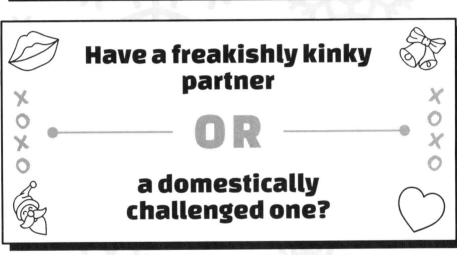

Have a freakishly kinky partner

OR

a domestically challenged one?

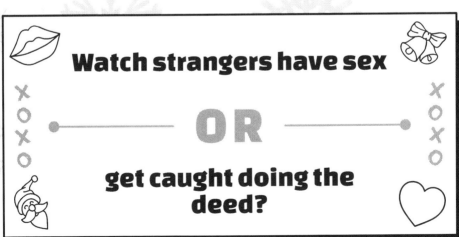

Watch strangers have sex

OR

get caught doing the deed?

WOULD YOU RATHER?

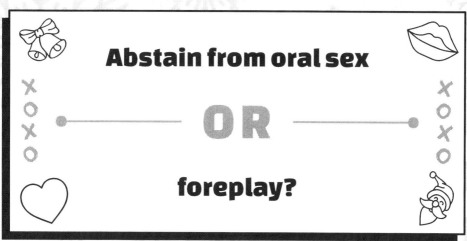

Abstain from oral sex

OR

foreplay?

Give up sex forever to maintain an appealing physical appearance you approve of

OR

have sex whenever you want to but dislike your appearance?

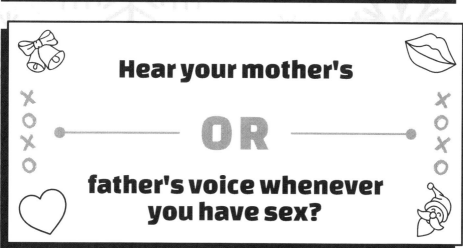

Hear your mother's

OR

father's voice whenever you have sex?

WOULD YOU RATHER?

Have mediocre sex with a faithful partner

OR

intensely pleasurable sex with someone who is promiscuous?

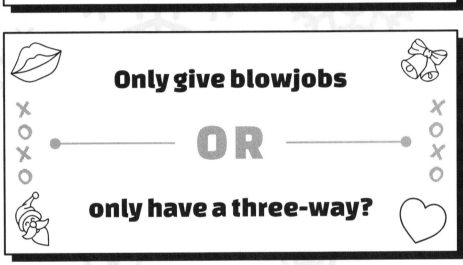

Only give blowjobs

OR

only have a three-way?

Be with a partner who only shaves their privates

OR

one who shaves everything except for their privates?

WOULD YOU RATHER?

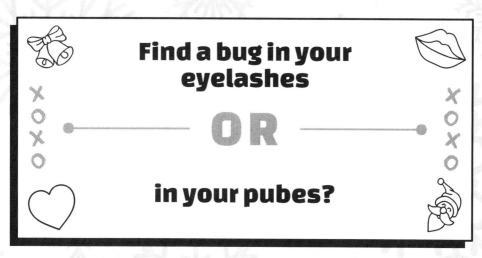

Find a bug in your eyelashes

OR

in your pubes?

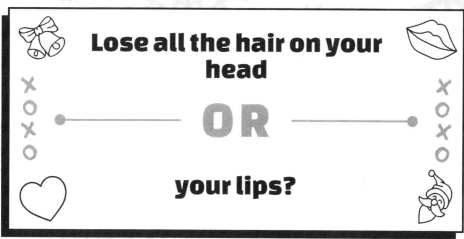

Lose all the hair on your head

OR

your lips?

Have fire ants in your pants

OR

poison ivy on your crotch?

WOULD YOU RATHER?

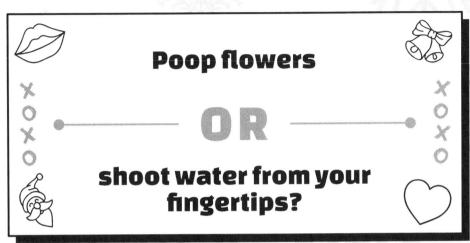

Poop flowers

OR

shoot water from your fingertips?

Be slapped by a dead fish

OR

swim in a pool full of cooked spaghetti?

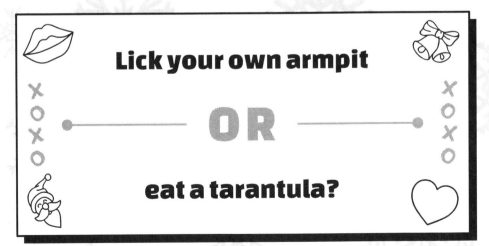

Lick your own armpit

OR

eat a tarantula?

WOULD YOU RATHER?

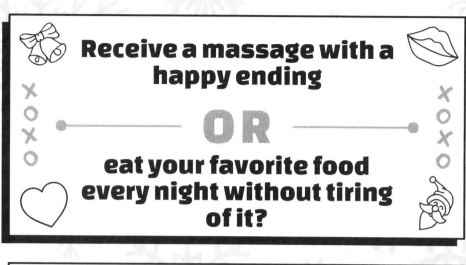

Receive a massage with a happy ending

OR

eat your favorite food every night without tiring of it?

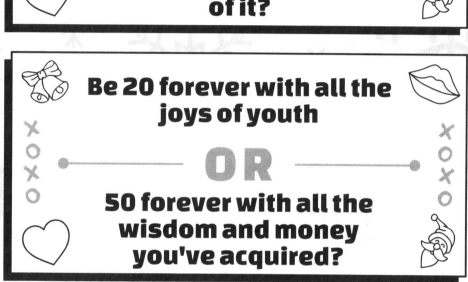

Be 20 forever with all the joys of youth

OR

50 forever with all the wisdom and money you've acquired?

Commit any crime without getting caught

OR

live forever?

WOULD YOU RATHER?

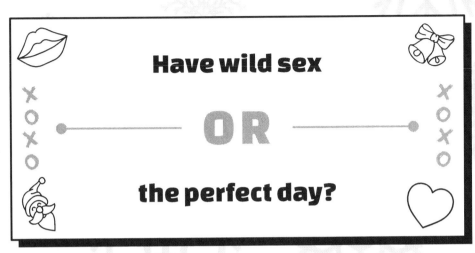

Have wild sex

OR

the perfect day?

Accidentally show your parents a naughty photo

OR

get butt-dialed and hear your parents having sex?

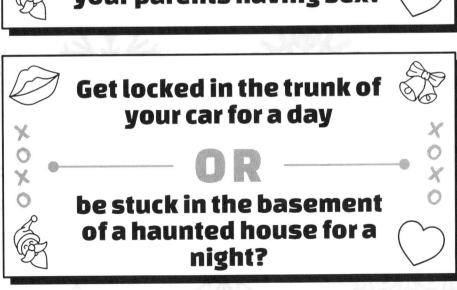

Get locked in the trunk of your car for a day

OR

be stuck in the basement of a haunted house for a night?

WOULD YOU RATHER?

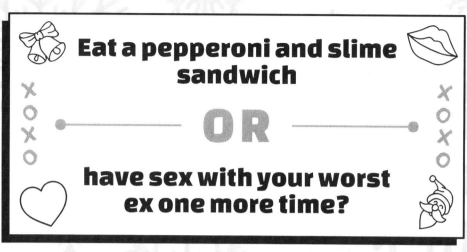

Eat a pepperoni and slime sandwich

OR

have sex with your worst ex one more time?

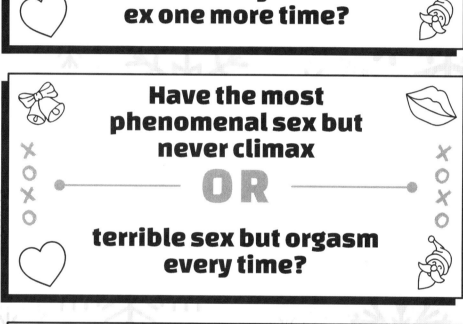

Have the most phenomenal sex but never climax

OR

terrible sex but orgasm every time?

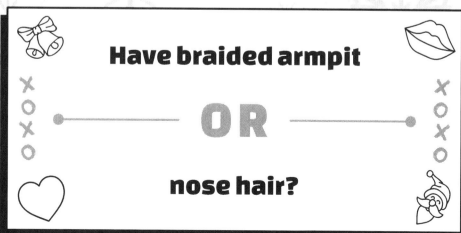

Have braided armpit

OR

nose hair?

WOULD YOU RATHER?

Give up coffee

OR

sex for a month?

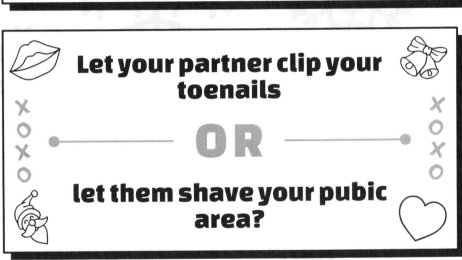

Let your partner clip your toenails

OR

let them shave your pubic area?

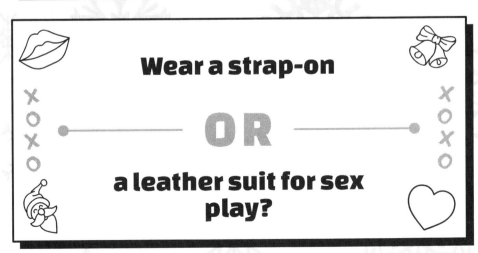

Wear a strap-on

OR

a leather suit for sex play?

WOULD YOU RATHER?

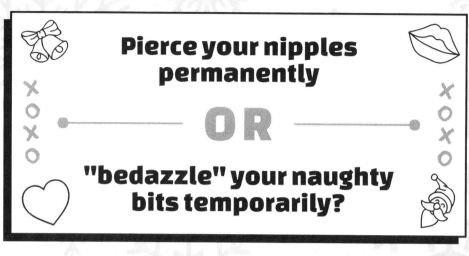

Pierce your nipples permanently

OR

"bedazzle" your naughty bits temporarily?

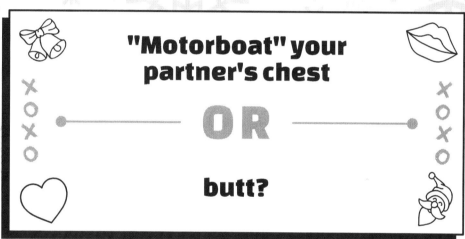

"Motorboat" your partner's chest

OR

butt?

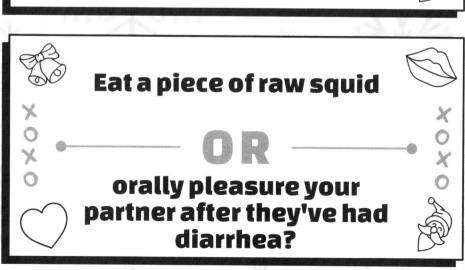

Eat a piece of raw squid

OR

orally pleasure your partner after they've had diarrhea?

WOULD YOU RATHER?

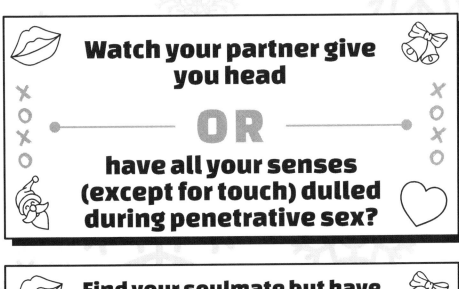

Watch your partner give you head

OR

have all your senses (except for touch) dulled during penetrative sex?

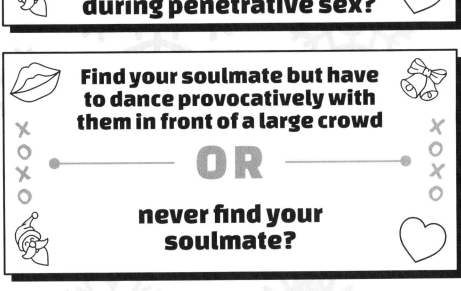

Find your soulmate but have to dance provocatively with them in front of a large crowd

OR

never find your soulmate?

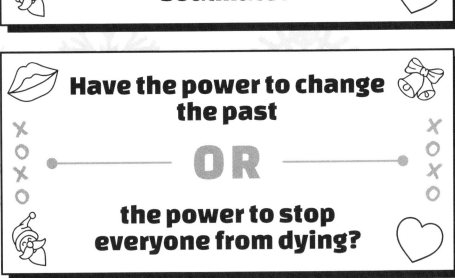

Have the power to change the past

OR

the power to stop everyone from dying?

WOULD YOU RATHER?

Be the little spoon while you cuddle with your partner

OR

drive with the seat adjusted to how your partner prefers it?

Have to dress up in a Halloween costume every day

OR

end every conversation saying, "Merry Christmas?"

Learn new skills by plugging your genitals into a computer

OR

be able to transfer your brain and everything about you into a new body?

Made in the USA
Monee, IL
13 December 2023

49153360R10055